Endlessly Passing

Also by Angela Johnson and published by Ginninderra Press
Neon Moons
No Stories, No Songs

Angela Johnson

Endlessly Passing

Acknowledgements

Some poems in this collection have been published in the following literary publications: *Blue Dog, Island, Poetrix, Five Bells, Eucalypt, Yellow Moon, The Mozzie,* the *Henry Kendall Anthology* 2012.

Some poems from *Neon Moons* (2004) are included, slightly changed.

'Bloodlines' was commended in the Henry Kendall award 2002 and published in the Central Coast Poets Anthology 2002 (*Bird Before Landing*).

'Wire Walls' 2005 and 'Dancing in Parlours' 2006 each won Poem of the Year in the Central Coast Poets Yearly Award.

I grew up in the years of the Great Depression. No doubt this has coloured my work. When I found Mature Age education in 1996, I was enthralled with an introduction to poetry.
I wished I'd found it sooner.

To all the poets I have met since I began my journey into this most testing of the arts, I say thank you for your willingness to share.

To Ginninderra Press, thank you for your support.

In memory of Clyde

Endlessly Passing
ISBN 978 1 74027 825 6
Copyright © text Angela Johnson 2013
Cover sketch of Gregory River: Angela Johnson
Cover design: Julie Wright

First published 2013
Reprinted 2016

GINNINDERRA PRESS
PO Box 3461 Port Adelaide SA 5015
www.ginninderrapress.com.au

Contents

Part one 7
  Endlessly Passing 9
  Embroidery 10
  Moonlight 11
  Sunlight 12
  Tanka 13
  Candle Wax 14
  Blood on the Path 15
  The Gardener 16
  Links 19
  The Fall 20

Part two 21
  Dancing in Parlours 23
  Closure 25
  Electricity Arrives 26
  Blue Walls 27
  Ribbons 28
  When I leave… 29
  The Verge 30
  Marked Words 31
  Tuesday Clouds 32
  Necklace 33

Part three 35
  Near Dorrigo 37
  A Distant Shimmer 38
  Time 40
  Boat People 1888 41

Bloodlines	42
South-west Victoria	43

Part four — 45

Blackout	47
With whom shall I dance	48
Sea Debris	50
Winter	51
The Sitter	52
Switch	53
Wire Walls	54
River Crossing	55
Sea Lover	56
Stalking	57
Soul	58
Walk to the Point	59
On the Fire Trail	61

Part five — 63

Tanka	65
The Thin Child Sings Bluebird of Happiness	66
Judgement	67
Albatross	68
A Tidy Man	69
Anonymity	70
African-born	72
Homeless	73
D.H. Lawrence in Etruria	74
Milk	76

Part one

Endlessly Passing

The green river flows under the dinghy. Its cool skin wraps the hull.

A favoured shirt is thin, stretched over strained shoulders.
Oars dip, pull the surface tension of the quiet river;
                                       arcing droplets glint.

Tall trees at the edge, drink slyly from water near the sedge
                                       the bow lays over.

Oars hang listless from the rowlocks, as

we step into clouds that swirl around our ankles
and a waterbird furls its wings, kisses its reflection.

Wattle drained of nectar drifts to grass-rimmed pools, caps our hair.

Endlessly the river passes lush paddocks, echoing hushing grain.

> *Rain has drawn circles on this river's face.*
>   *Death has lain on its bed.*
> *When you rowed in starlight*
> *I searched your shadowed face for certainty.*

Others row, long-stroked and rhythmic on the smooth water;
under the sun, under the moon and ever they row.

Birds in flocks land with mirrored wings on the welcome water

and we guide our craft over the wattle drifts, into the flow;
learn, there is no arriving or leaving on this journey.

Embroidery

My habitat ends
where the chicken wire fence
bends to an embroidery of

winding stems and a weight of leaves

behind which
someone else's small trees wince
before a tall tough grove
of eucalypts whose foliage

appliqués the edge of clouds.

Why then – on this late day
when the spool is running low –
do I think of you?

                      think of you…

A persistent image of your
grey garb; that green eyeshade
shattering light over your fine hands
stitching garments.

The secret scar on your mouth.

Why now do I grasp
your blood's warmth
in the warp and weft
of the cloth you handed me
                    was love?

Moonlight

strikes a note on the window
then you come questing again
no footfall – only a fitful shadow
trailing tunes.

From the hall
you falter at my door
ignore my greeting.
How should I name you?

Notions of ghosts or angels bewilder –
still
you are a presence and your melody
sounds like a requiem.

Sunlight

This morning I painted my nails
in the arms of the sun,
saw how it has followed me through days.
In its light I saw my hands afresh, ageing.

With a dog's patience, it will wait for my return.
Unless clouds intervene, it will touch me
from many angles, lend me a shadow.
When it tips below the trees, rosy light beguiles.

Tanka

night creeps
under the moon –
I dance
the eyes of the house
behind my back

small birds
under glass in museums
claws curled
how light they would be
on the palm of my hand

I avoid church
with the excuse
none are close by –
yet the memory of bells
tightens my throat

Candle Wax

pooled candle wax licks the rim
so many thoughts inhabit a room
a blue cup lasts another year
moonlight angles on the glass

so many thoughts inhabit a room
night is shuffling on the roof
moonlight angles on the glass
how long will the journey last

night is shuffling on the roof
boxes of leaves left on a shelf
how long will the journey last
all sap dries eventually

boxes of leaves left on a shelf
blackberries ripen on a stem
all sap dries eventually
I touch the memory of your skin

blackberries ripen on a stem
a blue cup lasts another year
I touch the memory of your skin
pooled candle-wax licks the rim.

Blood on the Path

When I tell you, invite you
into an image which follows my days
I note your querulous face;
your hand poised
over the next page of your book.

Instead, you could follow me
plunge your fingers
deep into the winding stems
of massed rose foliage on trellis;
breathe the fragrant red blooms;
feel the thick-cool of hidden dew.
                        Heed the prick.

See your blood on the path
sprinkled with yellow pollen?
It can't compete. Before bees arrive
rest your mouth on petals
smooth as the inside of lips.

The Gardener

Peach

1
He raised his hand to the globed fruit;
let the weight of it rest on his palm.

Each year of the tree's cycle,
from the first smother of pink blossom,
to the new grey furry buds,
he waited, as for a lover.

He watched the agitated hens
nurture the earth,
where he'd cast the grain.

The first pick was his.
He knew how it would be,
when the shape and colour
gave the nod.   A twist;

the heavy flesh around the small hard heart
leaving the branch,
suede skin, red as lust.

Inside the house it ripened in a bowl
until the fragrance invited consummation.

2
unexpectedly
she came to his bed
offering warmth –
moonlight on the quilt
stirred the planted seeds

3
the green sap
from stolen flowers
covered her hands
gracefully he pardoned
her indiscretion

4

Violets

Little sun reached
the windowless side of the house
where he planted violets.

He worked unseen
the cool-moist morning over him.
At night he slept like a priest.

Through the weatherboards
the sound of busyness
was an admonishment –

his girls
had grown their buds in secret
suddenly were women

who brought tea to his shed
pity in their eyes.

He stooped to the protective leaves,
stirred the earth with his fingers
revealed new furled blooms
bent on slender stems;

like his daughters as children
heads prayer-bowed for braiding
their bodies leaning in, the trust given.

Links

Between a ledge and the edge of a blind
a rectangle of light frames bare lattice

waiting for tendrils of jasmine
to twist through slats, coiling, winding.

Two sisters wind wool. One holds the skein apart,
flicks yarn to the other, who gentles it into a ball.

Between them a space of shared intimacy
is a confessional.

One speaks of cable stitch, a khaki garment
packaged yesterday, and how the stitch is like plaiting.

The other yearns for children;
                    daily braids her niece's hair.

The Fall

Camellias are flowering again.
They open and spill –

open and spill colour on the earth.

Thin petals, one upon the other
they fall, fragile as love.

Inside the house, there are many chairs
he uses one
and a small portion of the bed;

spurns warm covers – allows
the night air to cool him –

cool him like the jettisoned petals.

Part two

Dancing in Parlours

Aunts made heads turn –
dark hair free-falling
to the waist;
or springy red curls
and a snappy figure
made for high heels.

Aunts wore silky dresses
smoked cigarettes
in the manner of Garbo

travelled the world
in the darkness
of picture theatres

danced in parlours
to crooners
trapped in circles of shellac.

Aunts laughed out loud
open-mouthed
spread pleasure –
or cried private tears
into pillows at night;

always
expressed welcome
gave me portions of their pudding.

Aunts' houses were neat
the bed sheets smooth
a strange aloofness on my legs.

Aunts managed contraception
secretly: hushed conversations
a pale face in a single bed.

Aunts meddled with infidelity
the evidence in the face of a child;
or didn't, and played true
to the law of the pinny.

My aunts live forever.

Closure

The house awaits demolition.
No study or guest room with en-suite.

Yet once, in the breath of new timber,
a family managed the human huddle
with equanimity; kept separate
the tracks of their emotions.

A dormitory of lanky boys
crept between the ice-white sheets
of beds on a gauzed-in veranda
and slept to the grunt of distant cattle.

Sisters – privileged
in the intimacy of a shared room,
grew as different as their dreams.

The house seasoned to the clock's tick;
quivered to the thump of running feet;
the rhythmical slap of the screen door.

                Cigarettes lit, workers begin
                to rip weatherboards, and the flesh of walls
                to the blare of a truck's wireless.

                When they stop,
                the frame stands bare,
                and dust drizzles like rain
                on forgotten roses.

Electricity Arrives

Annie's house sparkled with electric light,
her kerosene lamps merely a decoration
their bowls coloured or clear – dried fringes
of wicks poking through metal slits.

The new light shone on the heavy polish
of furniture, on curlicues of wood, bounced
back from mirrors, made lush
                      a green velvet table cover.

***

Through our house, globes hung
fly-specked, unlit.
Hanging-cord switches were playthings,
the meter locked against
a shameful stack of unpaid bills.

So we lived by the lamp
its glass chimney dusted
by the smoke of an untrimmed wick;

and our shadows grew large on the walls,
danced around us, so eyes hid
in circles of dark, and the grey
bare house became softer in the night.

Blue Walls

She was curled
half foetal
her grey coat unwarm.

Newly painted
duck-egg blue walls
still showed the cracks.

His consoling arm
over her shoulders
was also a question.

They each believed
consent was legitimate
but her thoughts

were where their children lay
curled like kittens
in one large bed

with irredeemable coverings.

Ribbons

Memory flutters behind her
like ribbon on the wind.
Light and shade undulate
on peaks and troughs
of silken thread, unpicks
a bright brief moment.

A girl riding the cusp of youth.

Sunlight devours bare skin
and glints over a tumble of hair
swinging, spilling the scent of tea.

She watches herself

watching rowers from the bridge.
They are men.　　　　　　In summer
in the tea-tree nests at the beach
there had been kissing;

a clumsy dribble of bubbles on her face.

She looks again at the rowers
the torn surface of the water,
raises her hand. It is white and strong.
She could, she thinks, do anything.

When I leave…

When I leave this house tonight, I'll change
in a way unforeseen, return furtively
my face a veneer of sameness.

In preparation, in the bath, my limbs
strong and freckled, rock the scented water;
my small breasts, pink budded
are encircled by the warm water.

There is no full-length mirror to reflect
the virginal me – to reflect my nakedness.
I'm unprepared for a valuation of this self.

When light flits over structures flying past
and shrubs bend in the train's slipstream
home recedes. Distance lessens its influence;
dissipates the scented water.

The Verge

Grass crackles on the verge
of the road curving from memory

where we walked beneath a milk sky
our rhythm strong – in unison – until

a path invited us into the dim vault
of a pine forest.

Our muted footsteps quickened on the decline
our mouths wide with drying breath.

You reached out, pulled me beneath you
on the soft needled bed

where I felt the weight of your request.
I forget what I thought of your entering;

perhaps I reassessed your beauty. Later
I believed I'd become a woman – believed

I must stay with you always.

Marked Words

A surge of birdsong
rips open my reluctant morning.

In bed
we share our blood's warmth;
no plan to this touching and untouching.

Bedside, the page is still open
the words potent as before
and chafing at a new day.
My finger had marked each word
as I read to you, but your eyes glazed
as you hurried towards sleep.

        The text drowned in my mouth.

Your arm curves around my shoulders.
You ask, what is today's agenda?

Tuesday Clouds

Tuesday clouds
chase depth
from the rectangular shadows
of garden sheds.

On such a flat-air day –
also bereft of depth
and marble cold
I distanced myself.

Erased you
with less care
than I'd give to
a charcoal drawing

deaf to your grief
as words fell
like the dead heads of flowers

to the indifferent grass.

Necklace

Warm from my throat's flesh
links of twisted silver
coil their weight
in the cup of my hand.

A gift long ago
I forget the occasion
though I remember
my response was insouciant.

Now I see you
leave the mundane street
enter
a cave of gilt and glitter.

Under sharp lights
your fingers barely brush
the necklace spread on the glass
                      and you think of me.

Part three

Near Dorrigo

The valley is a dense, deep blue;
Fathomless.
There is no sound.
It's a moment
when forgiveness seems possible,
though frivolous
here, where far below, birds swim in circles
like spirits questing.

A Distant Shimmer

We weren't seeking it
the place that seemed
too small to call a town.

Low buildings
in middle-morning sun
placed on the flat dust
inviting roads, a name.

A signpost to elsewhere;
KLMS Oodnadatta track.

Fuelled-up we turn –
a pace unknown to
early surveyors
whose clip-clopping beasts
were company
making this red route.

The horizon is a shimmer
keeping its distance.

Corrugations rattled the truck
like a foxie with a rat.
Dust circumvented door seals
and seeped into our mouths.

Respite lay at the road's edge.

The car's engine ticked down.
Spilt water from our drinks
dried on contact with roadside rubble.

Looking out – nothing interrupted

the flat incandescent ochre earth;
no tree, no shrub, no bird –
no lengthening shadows
under a wide liquid sky.

Silence, pitiless and haunting.

How cold would the black night be?
How much light would the stars spill,
the moon pasting its cool light?

And the sun rising again, minute by minute
searing the endless stones.

And the early men who slept there
        to the gentle clink of hobbles.

Time

is a commodity we covet
as it rolls by time-lapsed
each square day filled/ciphered/
borrowed in advance
documented through the seasons.
So like a cornered mouse
my heart flutters seeking an exit
for a dark night near the Finke river
and the slow stars in a black sky.

Boat People 1888

(Families Garaventa and De Catania)

The air is gauze, coolly wrapped,
and a scent of recent flowers wafts
where this dormitory of sleepers
were tucked into eternity
an eternity ago.

Structures have softened:
are lichen-patterned and worn.
Down straight paths,
weeds' pink flowers quiver,
and crucifix shadows
twist in the sun.

(From all corners they sailed,
coerced by dreams or desperation;
felt a dumb resignation
as the hard earth rose to their first step;
      trailed like ants into their lives,
surprised at the tenacity of old bonds.)

Still, someone visits, owns these names,
wonders. Now rain speckles the stone,
gathers volume on a cold angel
and drips from the wing tips.

Bloodlines

Like any herd in fact, sheltered
in the dense shade of leaves and bracts,
they knew the value of a tree.

The blue checked shirts and moleskins
defined their breed
gathered there to talk bloodlines.

Their proper women spurn a uniform,
discreetly approach fashion's boundary,

confident in their genealogy of shared names,
through enhanced couplings, just like any herd.

South-west Victoria

1

They would have been small
in this vastness,
the men who planted these pines,
raking an alien earth,
becoming rootstock in a new land.

Now the rigid density
of windbreaks tames the space,
shelters their ghosts – repels
the southern ocean's wildness.

Subdued today
it brushes fields of barley,
whimpers around the car's windows.
        A mark on the map beckons.

2

We find a sun-brittle town.
Silent toy houses – a store; a locked pub
whose fibro structure belies the inscription,
Frenchman's Inn – eighteen forty-one.

Inside,
perhaps a remnant slab
of bluestone or framed old letters
will justify the claim.

The store is lean on stock –
mean with information.
We leave, rest by a boundary fence.
Already there is keening in the trees.

Part four

Blackout

The night the lights went out, we scrambled
blind as moles

and in the 'wink' when we found ourselves invisible
came the mantra

'I only believe what I see.'

Time ticked darkly – how long would it take
for your face to fade

like those from the past?

So I listened to gauge distance
by the rustle of your dress, your cautious breath.

On shuffling knees, I reached warily
into a cupboard

for wax candles.

Then I heard you fumble at the glass bowl
for a lighter

left beneath the flesh of fruit.

In fluttering candlelight
we remained on the floor

        were comforted at a soft-lit reality;
                the fresh slant of conversation.

With whom shall I dance

I said I wouldn't beg
should he want to leave.

When the time came
the sky was heading to indigo
shadows melting on the path.

All the people said
accept, he must go;

they all said
he has sailed oceans
he will know the way.

So I silenced my words
until sorrow filled my mouth
spilled out as questions.

Why when we're happy?
With whom shall I dance?
I knew the questions were trivial

from his patient smile
the sweep of his eyes
over all the people

who said he must go
who said to me, it's best for him.

His craft waited at the jetty
the oars unsecured.
I thought – throw them in the water.

(But I was awash with counsel.)

Quiet as air
he embarked and locked them in
and with his face blue

in the blue-dusk
left me with my fistful of trinkets.

Sea Debris

Shell and sea debris, pattern the transparency
of our shadows. The wind that snatches the sails
of yachts across the bay, snatches her hair
parts it evenly, as for plaiting.

Shoulders dipping, feet pooling sand,
she turns to where I stand. I expect to endure
cool scrutiny, but her glance reaches beyond me.
Again I package my guilt away. We watch a gull rise
its tucked red legs and oneness with the updraughts.

It's role reversal, for the trudge to firmer ground
when I reach for the cold bones of her hand.
Could I hold it to my breast, offer a late pittance of warmth?
Our palms part as she bends to a beach flower.

Winter

It's no use
blaming
the crumpled foil sea,
or the passive
dark clouds, hung low.

You lost your colours
long before this grey day.
See how the curious bird
points its yellow eye
in your direction? Look

at the way it spreads its wings
then lifts,
legs trailing,
and marks itself stark-white
between sea and sky.

The Sitter

You are unaware

lamplight defines your profile,
tips over your shoulder
and the rise of your breasts.

I prepare an imaginary canvas;
mix warm tones;
consider the rich glint of your bracelet.

I re-acquaint myself with your face,
background shadows in umber and violet
flicked with yellow; and your hands

that dark depth between fingers
the fragility of bone
the elusive journey of veins.

I've seen you hold a baby's head
the way you hold your book,
cupped in one hand.

The other is arced against your brow.
Then you look up – rise,
leaving me with a loaded brush.

Switch

This sibilant
frugal word,

pounces at random,
like a game of peek-a-boo.

Unlike
a melody that haunts,

spilling itself
in and out of you,

it has arrived suddenly;
brain embedded.

Switch:

interesting
rather than beautiful.

Definition: electric device:
no clue there.

Or, a thin bendable cane:
       has a rhythm to it.

Or, turning, shifting, changing:
            life's constant?

Switch:

to strike with a…

Wire Walls

Beneath low lamps we stitched garments.

My eyes avoided the white scar on your mouth
as I listened to your story, uncomprehending

a race spurned and branded
the blue numbers on your pale skin;

or the fetid reality in crowded carriages, where people,
crushed cargo, relinquished their dignity.

You did not speak, or could not
of the children, queued for their final bath-time.

You did speak, of the girl you had met through
wire-walls – of a promise.

                                With adolescent envy

I thought to compete; swirled around the factory
to Strauss on the wireless, a vernal display for you.

And when we met on the stairs, you held me
hard – breathed deep my tumbled hair;

brushed a soft dry kiss on my lips.
I thought it was like a movie.

Now that I know more, or less, I wonder
at the strength it took, to disavow the spat vitriol
                                          of 'Jude'

and I am humbled, when old dark-grained film
pans white-faced skeletons, hollow-eyed, gripping wire.

River Crossing

He is still, almost afloat
his body on the bed cool,
limbs straight, flesh and heart subdued.

He imagines the landscape
swaddled in cold,
the trees, petrified in the hush.

The muffled sound of the late night-train
nudges the air, winds to its inevitable journey
across the bridge, its metallic rhythm

reaching out, and down –
its windows, yellow flags
reflect in the dark river below.

He sees its passage;
few travellers, a driver and a guard,
and someone to exact the fare.

Sea Lover

Your voice is seductive,
a whisper
reaching my bed.

Other nights you moan;
edge towards torment
or rage at rock faces

dragging into you
the wet-edged earth
you must visit again
                      and again.

If I drown in you,
will you rock me forever?

Stalking

You could pass for a breeze
your trick-of-breath cooling my neck

as you follow.

You mime all shadows, the angles
and hollows of trees

but I know you are there.

How banal you are
with hooded garment and scythe

your yellow rictus grin.

Fashion is clearly not your thing
even when you appear on TV.

Deluded, I think you've come for me.

Soul

Do you call that soul, that thing
That chirps in you so timorously?
– Rainer Maria Rilke

Tell me,
how would I recognise it;
silent and invisible,
fraught with definitions, easy to doubt?

Abstractions puzzle me
but one I would share with you

is the way music flows
across space,

seeps into flesh with a theme
that means more
        than the sum
                of its parts.

How it folds around the viscera – tightens,
rises to where you think your heart is,
then throbs in your throat;

invites tears
to the rims of your eyes.

Walk to the Point

On the road to the point
up from the ragged road-metal edge
are many mansions, aspirational

now empty-eyed
as kept mistresses
above million-dollar views.

Against community expectation
a small house is painted
stark white with blue trim

and the road ends high above the sea
with a sign
'turning circle – no parking'.

The ocean roars, manic
over wind and tide
twists and clutches at the cliff

while down in Pittwater, two yachts
are slashes of white
erect before the wind.

Soon sailors' frantic hands
must turn the craft
judge the sails' geometry to heel.

This achieved, hearts quieten.
They point for home –
believe the elements beaten.

There will be no moon tonight.
Few windows will glow
but the sea will fold back on itself
sighing, languid in the dark.

On the Fire Trail

For Clyde

Stones skitter under a crush of boots.
Dust floats like smoke on the air.
Undeterred, the understory of boronia
gives birth to stems of pink blossom.

Grevillea, red as blood, hovers
over the little yellow suns of hibbertia.
How you loved to name them; count
their petals for verification.

At the summit, far above the Hawkesbury
you were rendered speechless
by its beauty.   Calm today
you would have empathised
with the drift of tiny yachts, edging out.
White birds on the tide.

Part five

Tanka

our hands
mine cold yours warm
touching –
how many years
have we lived with this?

the mower clatters
collecting gumnuts
and peeled bark –
the tree journeys
to winter mauve

you own me
I will stay with you always
wait on your word
you think I am sleeping
but my ears are pricked

The Thin Child Sings Bluebird of Happiness

Sylvie's place is on a corner and is still blue under sixty years of mould patterning the two-storey-high walls, with no sign of life at the main door, though there never was, as all exits and entrances happened through the narrow gate in the bluestone lane, with the squeaky hinges giving warning or welcome into a passageway to the stairs, adjacent to the always dark room, with a light shade hovering over a pool table, illuminating disembodied hands thrusting cues at balls; or lighting up part of a smoke-wreathed profile, as the thin child watched surreptitiously while waiting for Sylvie. She wondered which of the myriad shaped legs in stockings burst at the seams, or gathered around bony ankles of women alighting the stairs, belonged to her friend's mother who provided the sandwiches they ate together in the mean yard, beside a pot plant hanging grimly to a remnant of green, like Sylvie's eyes watching.

The thin child was in awe that her friend took dancing lessons and had a smart haircut, so, as well as the sandwiches, she accepted more largesse by way of a top hat and tails, to aid her own performance at the school concert, though she hadn't considered that she was thin and Sylvie fat; therefore the trousers had to be gathered at the waist while the legs were half mast, as she stood motionless in front of the class singing a ballad, that had no use for a top hat and cane, in spite of which her voice rose as high and as sweet as a bird.

Judgement

Inside the house where you once lived
where walls of flowers trailed and bloomed
where dreams were patched, hope retrieved
your happiness had been assumed.

It was your back on those cold sheets
and duty heavy on your breast.
The consequence lay at your feet.
Did you believe that you were blessed?

A journal lying in a drawer
gave a clue, words full of grace.
Beneath the text, a space left for
a naïve sketch of each child's face.

Then from my throat a sob of air
how could I know who was not there.

Albatross

The wind rebuffs our passage
and our shoes slip in pools of sand.
The dunes are low, tea-tree tangled.

I fear the sea; its insistent tug
the smothering wallow in its depth.

Today, dark slate, it reaches the horizon
under thin bleached clouds.
At the shore it reclaims itself.

The green waves at the beck of the tide
leave a dry line of salt-foam
lace patterned with curled edges.

Here, is recent death, sudden at our feet
no clue to its passing, no thing to blame.

Ballet-legs twist under fine wings
and the empty eye socket, a dark tunnel
travels in to an intricate mass
                              of bones and flesh.

We look back – measure our journey
then take an exit track, to the shelter of trees.

A Tidy Man

Surely there was little strength
in his timid fingers on the glass
held by the dry tips
lifted archly to pursed lips.

The dainty sip;

a slow circumspect return
to the cloth; no prints on the glass.
When, by virtue of a smile – he revealed
a rabble of teeth I drew my scarf
around the stem of my throat.

Anonymity

The last seat
and the question of drink settled
he relaxed to the rhythm of the train.

In burglar-black the dark skin
of his face gleamed beneath a beanie
his hands, bronze, emerged from long sleeves.

He leaned forward
full lips froth speckled.

'Once I saw a dead man in a pub.
The police came, and I was afraid.
I was under age.'

Mock concern was my option.
Reduce his confession
to the realm of fairy tale;

but the stories spilled like a net
casting me as conspirator,
each ending in an admission
of some minor crime.

Now darkness
leaning against the window
reflected our image
        our eyes meeting there.

The express rattled on
the stories, honed I guessed
over many journeys, were endless.
He nameless.

He opened a fresh bottle.
Eyes glazed he swilled,
wiped his mouth with his hand.

Disembarking passengers queued.
Taking my chance I stood, gripped
the metal handle on the seat's back.

A Judas, I smiled at his final words.
'You're a good woman.'

African-born

Compliant,
your big eyes
in a shrivelled face
look into the camera.

Too young
to have learned expectation,
you suck
at empty breasts.

A rag,
a shroud, hangs
from your stick arm,
thin hand clasping mother's flesh.

What is our sympathy to you?
You would not recognise it.
Hovering-death
is more honest than our tears.

Soon you will lie
diminutive
in a row of mummies.

Your legacy;
A face beamed around the world.

Homeless

After Job 30:15

Fear follows me:
It has wrenched at my soul.
Comfort has flown on the wind.
I sense my soul is leaving
as my ageing controls me.
At night my bones scream
and my flesh burns.
My twisted body is repellent
for I am swaddled in disease
and cast aside
soon to become ashes.
I cry out to the sky, I am unheard;
I struggle abroad, I am invisible.

D.H. Lawrence in Etruria

I'd know you anywhere, your cadaver face, rough beard
your tousled hair.

At a distance on a crisp morning, I follow you to Cervetiri
from where the distant sea is a bright knife, and Tumuli

stretch toward the mountains.

In Rome you prowled museums, your eyes fire;
scribbled notes, derided the Romans.

'Prussians of the Etruscan Demise'.

Entering the tombs, in crumbling passageways
you stumble behind the guide
dense shadows folding in behind the hiss and glare

of his acetylene lamp; you breathe the sour earth,
tremble at your quest realised.

Etruscan Man's red-painted nakedness appeals to you.
Over and again you return to it. He is divine.

His fair women, clothed in blue cotton, are regal, quiescent.
I remind myself, this is your interpretation.

Aren't you deterred by these endless graves?
Already your lungs weep for death: or is that it?

The fairy tale belief of the Etruscans, that a happy life
continues in the hereafter; as though it were a new thought.

I'm weary of these ravaged dead,
the philosophy of the phallus, this clever prose.

Write me fields of flowers,
living paragraphs of colour, delicacy and scent;
the rhythm of the seasons.

I trail behind on soft, fruitful grasses, find you again
in Volterra, where ash-chests are many.

As this journey ends, exhaustion is your shroud,
skin translucent as marble.

Tumuli: grassy mounds over Etruscan graves.
Lawrence was suffering from tuberculosis.
Ash-chests: marble containers for remains.

Milk

Today the sky is milk.
It pours over my garden
fills buckets to the brim.

I could run unclothed
bathe in its warmth
open my mouth

        and drink my fill.

Instead, I return to my room
where light spills white on walls
slakes my thirst of days

so I can write these words.

www.ingramcontent.com/pod-product-compliance
Lightning Source LLC
Chambersburg PA
CBHW062151100526
44589CB00014B/1777